TRAIL OF THE OLD MAN

Historical and Legendary Stories of
New Hampshire's

Old Man of the Mountain

PAUL D. BERUBE

TABLE OF CONTENTS

a. INTRODUCTION and ACKNOWLEDGMENTS
b. ABOUT THE AUTHOR
c. POETIC INTRODUCTION

1. THE ARRIVAL OF THE OLD MAN
2. THE NEW SETTLERS
3. THE RESCUE
4. TIME MOVES ON
5. THE FATAL FALL
6. THE SCIENTIFIC TIME LINE
7. A MESSAGE IN STONE
8. AN INDIAN LEGEND
9. THE LEGEND OF MANITOU
10. GRANDFATHER'S TALE
11. AN UNKNOWN LEGEND
12. TRAIL OF AN OLD WARRIOR
13. THE LEGEND OF A SAGAMORE
14. THE RETURN OF WHITE DOVE
15. IN THE OLD MAN'S PRESENCE
16. THE WARRIOR'S DREAMS
17. THE INDIAN HEAD
18. THE IMPRUDENT EAGLE
19. ALL TRAILS LEAD TO HIS HOME
20. AT HIS TRAILS END
21. SHELTER FROM THE STORM
22. THE WATCHER
23. PROFILES, BOULDERS AND ROCK FORMATIONS
24. A MODERN DAY LEGEND
25. A TEACHER OF STONE
26. A TRAIL OF REMEMBRANCE
27. ALIVE IN OUR HEARTS AND SOULS

INTRODUCTION and ACKNOWLEDGEMENTS

High above the lush valley which makes up Franconia Notch, the gateway to northern New Hampshire, there lived an old man. He has been described as a relentless tyrant, a fantastic freak, and a learned philosopher, feeble of mind and weak of mouth and of unique beauty, most stern and very solemn, one of the most remarkable wonders of the mountain world.

Daniel Webster once said, "Men hang out their signs indicative of their respective trades; shoe makers hang out a gigantic shoe; jewelers a monster watch, and the dentist hangs out a gold tooth; but up in the mountains of New Hampshire, God Almighty has hung out a sign to show that there He makes men."

And, so it happened that New Hampshire had its Profile, "The Old Man of the Mountain," beautifully outlined against the western sky; a sign so unique, distinctive and inspirational as to the kind of men the sons of the Granite State should always long to be.

The Old Man of the Mountain had several names including "The Profile", "The Great Stone Face", "The Old Man," and "The Old Man of the Mountain."

The Profile was composed of Conway red granite and was actually an illusion formed by five ledges, that when lined up correctly, gave the appearance of an old man with an easterly gaze, clearly distinct and visible from only a very small spot near Profile Lake. When viewed from most any other location in Franconia Notch, the same five ledges had a very rough and haphazard appearance, and there was no suggestion of The Profile of the Old Man of the Mountain.

Geological opinion was that The Profile on Cannon Mountain was supposed to have been brought forth partly as the result of the melting and slipping away of the ice sheet that covered the Franconia Mountains at the end of the glacial period, and partly by the actions of the frost and ice in crevices, forcing off and moving certain rocks and ledges into the positions that created the profile. It has been suggested that the Old Man of the Mountain was completed during the latter part of the post glacial period, from 2,000 to 10,000 years ago.

The Old Man was formed on the side of Cannon Mountain, which juts out abruptly into open air, approximately 1200 feet above Profile Lake. It was made up of five layers of granite ledge, one just above the other, the total distance being 25 feet. Of these five ledges one formed the chin, another formed the upper lip, a third the nose and two ledges made up the entire forehead. The Old Man has been measured as being forty feet, five inches in height.

I would first like to thank the Old Man of the mountain himself for giving me the inspiration to write this book. Without the wisdom and friendship he has given me over the many years I have known him, this book would not have been possible.

I would also like to thank all the kind folk at the Moultonboro Public Library for the help they gave me during my research concerning the Great Stone Face. Their aid in helping me find the legends and stories about the Old Man were invaluable. To my wife, Joanne, of course, who offered me her support, patience, understanding and criticism. Thank you also goes to Christine Alwin, my most professional and harshest critic. To all my dedicated readers, I thank you for your continued support and encouraging letters and emails.

I dedicate this book to my youngest son Jonathan. Jon was not yet 4 years old when The Old Man came crashing down in 2003. He saw The Old Man of the Mountain when he was just three and half years old but has no recollection of that experience. I hope that this book will forever etch a vision of The Old Man in his mind and help him to understand just what the Old Man meant to so many people from all over our the world.

ABOUT THE AUTHOR

Born in Fall River, MA in 1952, Paul grew up in Somerset, MA; a small town across the Taunton River. He lived in Somerset until 1994 and then moved to Cranston, Rhode Island close to the Roger Williams Park and Zoo. In March of 2001, Paul moved to Meredith, New Hampshire with his wife, Joanne, and their then 21 month old son Jonathan. Paul and his family now reside in the town of Moultonboro, NH; a small, picturesque town on the northeast shores of Lake Winnipesaukee. Paul has also been blessed with four other children, ages twenty four through thirty two, who now reside in Pennsylvania, Massachusetts, Michigan and Rhode Island.

After the World Trade Center tragedy of September 11, 2001, Paul felt the need to do more, so he joined the local on-call volunteer fire department and graduated from the New Hampshire Fire Academy as a Pro Board Accredited Firefighter in March of 2003. At about the same time, Paul was approached by an Army National Guard recruiter and asked about his military background. That June, he was once again sworn into the Guard and soon received orders to report to Fort Sill, OK for re-training. Due to Paul's debilitating arthritic condition however, he was found to be unfit for deployment overseas and was given a second Honorable Discharge in March of 2004. Paul received his first Honorable Discharge in August, 1981 after serving in the Massachusetts Army National Guard for 10 years as FDC Chief with Delta Battery 1/211 Field Artillery out of Fall River.

At 56 years old, Paul decided to return to college to pursue a degree in law. He is currently attending classes at Hesser University in Concord, NH and is looking forward to transferring to the Massachusetts School of Law at Andover to obtain his law degree.

Unfortunately, due to joint replacement surgery, he no longer serves as an on call Firefighter. But Paul hopes that through his poetic story telling, he can still help others in some small way.

Paul is the author of four other books of poetic stories. His first book, TRAIL'S END POETRY, Lessons in Life, was published in June 2007. He followed this up with MOUNTAIN TRAILS, Lessons in Life - Book 2, in October, 2007 and then in January, 2009, came TRAILS TO ETERNITY, Lessons in Life - Book 3. In March, 2009, after a year and a half in the making, came GENESIS DECODED, The Biblical Trails of Lessons in Life - Book 4.

POETIC INTRODUCTION

High above Franconia Notch,
Lived a man sent down from above;
There to watch over a valley,
Sent to us with The Spirit's love.

The man was known by many names,
Like "The Profile" and "The Old Man;"
Also known as "The Great Stone Face,"
And, "The Old Man of the Mountain."

He'd been described as a tyrant,
A learned philosopher too;
Also called a fantastic freak,
His nicknames were more than a few.

Created from red granite rock,
Ever gazing out to the east;
Sublimely outlined in the sky,
An imposing sight to say the least.

Some said he was an illusion,
Just a freak of nature at best;
Created during an ice age,
Some thought of him as even less.

History tells many stories,
Too many for me to tell of;
You must draw your own conclusion,
To me, he was placed there with love.

Chapter 1

THE ARRIVAL OF THE OLD MAN

Perched at the very top of the mountain,
The Spirit sent him to watch over man;
He looked around for just the right place,
To settle down and devise a plan.

He had been sent here on a mission,
That had to be done both day and night;
To constantly watch over mankind,
The spot he would choose had to be right.

With no idea where this trail would lead,
Or how long he would be asked to stay;
He'd need a place both high and open,
To weather storms and see every way.

He found a spot just above a lake,
A perfect place to set up his home;
For untold days and nights he would sit,
Knowing he had to do this alone.

Now this was the time of early man,
Well before the Indian hunters;
His duty was simple at the start,
He relaxed and enjoyed the wonders.

Then one day new settlers came 'round,
They noticed the man perched up high;
All made a special kinship with him,
They called him Old Stone Face in the sky.

Those who knew him felt he was special,
Felt that he had The Spirit within;
And if He had placed Old Stone Face there,
Was He keeping a log of their sin?

The word soon traveled both far and wide,
About this old man who lived alone;
On top of the mountain called Cannon,
Why had he chosen it for his home?

His presence could be felt from below,
A higher power was raining down;
His face was etched as if in deep thought,
Some swore they could see sweat on his brow.

The Old Man proved to be about love,
Just ask all those who come to his place;
Heavenly essence of peace and love,
Radiated from that old stone face.

Chapter 2

THE NEW SETTLERS

As the years passed many people came,
To catch a view of the old stone face;
Many decided to stick around,
And settled near this majestic place.

The rich valley had much to offer,
With natural springs and fertile ground;
Abundant timber for sturdy homes,
Natural wonders, they did abound.

Before too long a new town was built,
New industries began to flourish;
Beneath the shadow of the Old Man,
They found that all their needs were nourished.

The settlers soon began to believe,
The Spirit had sent Old Stone Face here;
For surrounding forests were teeming,
With life giving food like white tailed deer.

Lakes and ponds were in great abundance,
An endless supply of fish they gave;
New people moved here from miles around,
New immigrants felt they had been saved.

Soon the valley filled up with thousands,
More and more folks built new log homes;
With the Old Man looking down on them,
One never felt that they were alone.

The Old Man could plainly be seen,
From miles away almost any day;
With sunshine enhancing his features,
It was hard to turn one's eyes away.

As more people kept coming to see,
What all of the ruckus was about;
And once they looked at his mighty face,
They said, "The Spirit sent him, no doubt."

Chapter 3

THE RESCUE

The years went by very quickly,
The industrial age was at hand;
People the world over had heard,
Of the mountain with its Old Man.

The horseless wagon made its debut,
To travel far was now so easy;
The people who lived in the valley,
Built a new road so that all could see.

The majestic stone face up high,
They wanted the whole world to know;
How he was looking over them,
And their town continued to grow.

Soon after that someone took notice,
That the Old Man was losing his grip;
Some stones around his foundation,
They were slowly starting to slip.

His neighbors came to his rescue,
Just to help him is what they craved;
His spirit was so much alive,
They knew the Old Man must be saved.

They climbed to the top of Cannon,
Walked to the edge above his home;
Without much thought for their safety,
They struggled to reinforce the stone.

And they returned year after year,
They helped keep the Old Man alive;
With stones and cables they held him,
They wouldn't let Old Stone Face die.

The love that he had brought with him,
Rained down on those living below;
The meaning of his presence here,
Was quickly beginning to grow.

Chapter 4

TIME MOVES ON

During the industrial age,
Stories of the Old Man spread more;
Some were fact and others legends,
Still, the people enjoyed his lore.

A highway was built through the notch,
That soon became an interstate;
Huge trucks created vibrations,
Pollution came to Profile Lake.

No longer a lush, green valley,
His sight was made a tool for greed;
Simply to lure more tourists in,
Soon piranha began to feed.

Vibrations crept through the mountain,
Moving a pebble at a time;
Creating cracks across his home,
His foundation no longer prime.

Despite all of their best efforts,
To hold The Profile in its place;
It was just a matter of time,
Before we'd lose sight of his face.

And the Old Man sent messages,
Like The Spirit's, they fell on deaf ears;
All of the warnings were ignored,
Some days you could see his tears.

Now, a piece of our history,
Would soon come to a bitter end;
People would come to see him and ask,
"What has happened to our old friend?"

Chapter 5

THE FATAL FALL

Was dark and early that morning,
On May Third, Two Thousand and Three;
The ground started to slowly shift,
His foundation was breaking free.

The sun hadn't even risen,
When the mountain started to quake;
The Old Man's life line was slipping,
As the perch he loved began to shake.

He held the mountain with all his might,
The earth was stronger, he felt it slide;
Campers below heard the fatal crash,
As The Old Man took his final ride.

Daylight came; they knew he was gone,
When they looked up all they could see;
Was broken rock and his empty ledge,
He wasn't there where he used to be.

No one needed to lower their eyes,
Knowing all that remained of the man;
Was bits of gravel near Profile Lake,
Sadly, all mourned the loss to their clan.

Yet his spirit will always live on,
In the hearts of all those that know;
The body crumbles but not the soul,
Love from his home continues to flow.

For those who will still stop and look,
At the mountain where he used to be;
As plain as day, the Old Man's still there,
This is the way it was planned you see!

Chapter 6

SCIENTIFIC TIME LINE

600 to 170 BC

An ice cap was drawing away,
From what's now known as New England;
Creating rivers, pond and lakes,
And all its majestic mountains.

And sometime during all those years,
The Old Man was carved out of stone;
Perched on the side of Cannon Mountain,
For more than two thousand years, his home.

1604 AD

The American Indians,
Had a legend that did describe;
A mountain with a great stone face,
This was known to many a tribe.

Follow the Merrimack River north,
When you enter the narrow valley;
Look upward towards the setting sun,
A great stone face is what you will see.

1805

Some groups of surveyors were working,
In Franconia Notch, as it's known;
Several claimed to discover him,
Atop the mountain that was his home.

But credit for his discovery,
Is given to two, Brooks and Whitcomb;
Since then the Old Man of the Mountain,
Would never spend a day all alone.

1905

Reverend Guy Roberts of Whitefield,
Took notice that the Man's forehead stone;
Had begun to slip off the mountain,
Sought help in saving the Old Man's bones.

He went to the owner of the Notch,
Colonel Greenleaf was a decent man;
They agreed that they had a problem,
They needed to come up with a plan.

The Army Colonel didn't know how,
The minister didn't have a clue;
But they began to search for a fix,
Someone who'd know just what to do.

1915

The Reverend then found Edward Geddes,
From Quincy, MA who worked with granite;
He had an idea of what to do,
And he wasted no time to plan it.

He'd used a device in the quarries,
The turnbuckle was a simple tool;
He was selected to do the job,
"Let's save the Old Man," became the rule.

The money needed to fund the work,
It came from the people of the state;
The turnbuckles were made in Vermont,
That would soon decide the Old Man's fate.

1916

Roberts, Geddes and four helpers came,
To work upon the Old Man's head;
Geddes worked from sunrise to sunset,
To save the Man from certain death.

As a result of his hard work,
The fingers on one of his hands;
Fell victim to severe frostbite,
And for life, disfigured the man.

But again, because of his work,
The stone has hardly moved at all;
Many decades it stayed that way,
Ed had delayed the Old Man's fall.

1925

But now the owners wanted to sell,
Six thousand acres and the Old Man;
Money for its preservation came;
From everywhere to buy that land.

1928

A special day of dedication,
It becomes a State Forest and Park;
To save the Old Man of the Mountain,
On Cannon in Franconia Notch.

1937

Ed Geddes makes his last trip to see,
Visits the Old Man one more time;
Takes measurements but nothing's changed,
The Old Man is doing just fine.

He places cinder blocks in a crack,
So anyone can tell if he's moved;
The Old Man of the Mountain lives on,
And to his rescuers he's behooved.

1945

The Old Man of the Mountain becomes,
The official emblem of the state;
A great symbol of Live Free or Die,
Now world renowned is The Old Man's fate.

1950

Inspected once again this year,
No problems found, nothing is wrong;
No work is even conducted,
The Old Man is solid and strong.

1954

Again an inspection is done,
The crack that Geddes had spoken of;
Opened a fraction of an inch,
The Old Man needs more care and love.

1955

The legislature introduces,
A bill to spend nearly twenty grand;
The bill passes in Fifty Seven,
To again, revive the Old Man.

1958

Repairs are again underway,
Four more turnbuckles atop his head;
Led by a man named Stanton Young,
A ditch is dug to prevent his death.

1960

Niels F. F. Nielsen Jr,
A worker on the state highways;
Dedicates over thirty years,
To saving that old Great Stone Face.

Becoming the First Official,
Caretaker of the great Old Man;
Without his love and fortitude,
Not for long could the Profile stand.

1960 - 1965

Annual checks of The Old Man,
Were done by a determined clan;
Led by a good man named Dolph Bowles,
They'd be found working hand in hand.

1965

Work party made up of family,
And volunteers from the mountain staff;
Risking their lives for the Great Stone Face,
Praying while working to hold it fast.

1969

The first trip up for David Nielsen,
To give The Old Man a haircut and shave;
Dave worked on The Old Man ever since,
Passed down from his Dad, The Old Man to save.

He became the Second Official,
Caretaker of the Great Old Stone Face;
With help from a university,
Seismology studies soon took place.

1971

Niels descends the face of The Old Man,
His first time using of a boatswain's chair;
This is the first close up inspection,
Of the south and front of The Man's beard.

1972

A crack is then sealed on the south face,
With a membrane of wire, glass and cloth;
This covered up The Old Man's right ear,
A bit more time the caretakers bought.

1973

Niels installs fourteen numbered tags,
Across the front of the Old Man's face;
To properly measure any movement,
The next ten years there's nary a trace.

1976

And then in Nineteen Seventy Six,
Dave makes his first trip over the edge;
His first time over the Old Man's face,
Then in Eighty he does it with Dad.

1983

Then Deborah Goddard makes her first trip,
On a date with David to the Old Man;
They're married in Nineteen Eighty Four,
Now partners on and off the mountain.

1988

Deborah becomes the first woman,
Over the edge of the Old Man;
And also their young son Thomas,
Made his first trip with all the clan.

1989

Niels makes his final trip to the Man,
By helicopter he was flown there;
He said his goodbyes and then flew off,
Left him in Dave and Deborah's care.

1990 - 1991

David and others descend his face,
To inspect The Man's "Adam's Apple;"
They find that there are problems with it,
Come up with a plan but must be careful.

In nineteen ninety one it is fixed,
The Old Man is like new again;
Technology and a bit of glue,
Have once again saved their old friend.

1991 - 2001

Annual inspections occur,
And the measurements have not changed;
Over this ten year period,
All of them are exactly the same.

2001 - 2002

Sadly in Two Thousand and One,
Niels F. F. Nielsen passed away;
Some of his ashes gently placed,
Buried in the Old Man's left eye.

2003

On May Third of this fateful year,
They say he succumbed to a quake;
His remains forever at rest,
Far below, close to Profile Lake.

On May Sixth, then Governor Benson,
Establishes an Old Man Task Force;
And a Revitalization Fund,
In tribute to the Old Man of course.

On May Tenth they hold their first meeting,
And a Family Remembrance Day;
It is held in Franconia Notch,
Young and old come to reflect and pray.

2009

This brings us to the present day,
And though the Old Man has parted;
A tribute will soon be built for him,
In the place where his legend started.

Chapter 7

A MESSAGE IN STONE

I went by his old home today,
For a thought had come to my mind;
About why the Old Man is gone,
An interesting tale you'll find.

But I'd like to take just a moment,
To quote what Daniel Webster once said;
Exactly why the Old Man was there,
Why we were so blessed to see his head.

"Men hang out their signs indicative,
Of their respective trades;
Shoemakers hang out a gigantic shoe;
Jewelers a monster watch,
And the dentist hangs out a gold tooth.

But in the mountains of New Hampshire,
God has hung out a sign to show;
That it is there that He makes men."
And he wanted us all to know.

The point to my theory is this,
When a tradesman closes his door;
Never to open it again,
He takes down his sign, forevermore.

I think that God had reached that point,
He simply got fed up with us;
For many have turned Him away,
In God, they no longer place their trust.

I think that He took down His sign,
Reluctantly, took it away;
While trying to sort mankind out,
Whether to grant us another day.

Now, I wouldn't blame Him at all,
Should He take all His blessings back;
For we've become a wicked lot,
Don't kid yourself, you know it's fact.

A great nation this country was,
By God, all our morals were set;
But mankind has become too proud,
Pride is a sin, less we forget.

It's time we got back to basics,
But I think it may be too late;
For God has taken His sign down,
Now what I fear for, is our fate.

The Old Man was taken back home,
And he's in a much better place;
I thank God for the memories,
Through His love I still see Stone Face.

The loss of our beloved Old Man,
May simply be another sign;
Not the one we've been waiting for,
None the less, a sign that it's time.

A sign that it's time for changes,
To make this country strong again;
It's time we *mean* "IN GOD WE TRUST,"
A message from an old, dear friend.

The sign of the Old Man is gone,
But still, he left us a message;
"Return to the ways God taught you,
When He made you in His image."

Chapter 8

ONE INDIAN LEGEND

Now Indian legend tells us,
A totally different story;
Of how the Old Man came to be,
In all his majestic glory.

Ulala was Chief of his tribe,
That dwelled in the fortressed valley;
He took great care of his people,
Loving and paternal was he.

But then one day the white man came,
Up from where they lived in the south;
Brought death and destruction with them,
Trying to drive his people out.

The Indian Chief sadly watched,
For there was nothing he could do;
Against their weapons that spewed fire,
The survivors were very few.

He climbed the side of the mountain,
And looked down with a tearful eye;
At his people's retreating forms,
When the battle was done, he cried.

His tears fell down the mountain side,
And formed the tiny lake beneath;
As Ulala stood at the ledge,
All at once, his breath simply ceased.

His lips became rigid as rock,
And then his forehead grew stone cold,
Ulala's features were transformed,
Into the Great Stone Face of old.

Chapter 9

THE LEGEND OF MANITOU

Another Indian legend tells of,
The Mohawks who called him Manitou,
They prayed he'd protect their homes,
Help them to get through life somehow.

One day while retreating from a raid,
Returning up the winding Notch trail;
Exhausted, they camped in the valley,
Below the ledge where Manitou hailed.

At sunrise they noticed the great face,
Frowning on them from up in the sky;
As they fell down on their knees in fear,
They heard the dreaded Manitou cry.

"You have made war on your brothers,
Their blood's on your hands and yet;
You dare come to the Great Spirit,
Unsummoned, the penalty is death."

Lulled by a strange spellbinding song,
They just laid trembling on the ground;
They fell asleep and turned to stone,
As huge boulders, they're still found.

Chapter 10

GRANDFATHER'S TALE

The year was Nineteen Fifty Seven,
Grandfather bought his first new car;
Most every day he'd go for a ride,
Sometimes his rides would take him far.

He went for a ride to New Hampshire,
For he wanted to get his first look;
At the profile of the Old Man,
He found a peaceful spot by a brook.

Where he could sit down and reminisce,
Of stories he'd heard about Stone Face;
Both his Mom and Dad used to tell him,
He's a sign God's been to this place.

He sat there and was thinking about,
Historic legends of the Old Man;
All at once he heard a soft whisper,
Felt something softly brush his hand.

He looked to his right, and saw nothing,
Turned around, there was nobody there;
He glanced to his left, not a soul around,
But he felt a strange presence in the air.

He shook it off as a trick of the wind,
Turned back to the mountain once more;
'Fore he remembered where he'd left off,
It happened again, the same as before.

Now his mind was working rapidly,
There had to be an explanation;
Was he beginning to lose his mind,
Or were his senses on vacation.

Without so much as another thought,
He began to get ready to leave;
He stood and started to walk away,
When he felt someone tug at his sleeve.

He turned to find an old Indian,
Smiling at him with a toothless grin;
He said, "Sit down and we'll talk awhile,
About that stone with the Spirit within."

He told him about a legend of lore,
An old story that was passed to him;
That God put the face on the mountain,
To watch over mankind's foolish whims.

He said, "The Spirit lives in the rock,
Passes His flame to the hearts of men;
To give them courage within their souls,
To walk on the trails that God planned.

"But over all the years that have passed,
God's patience with man started to thin;
And he may remove the face to show us,
Without faith in God, the devil will win."

And then the old Indian was gone,
Without so much as a quick 'goodbye;'
But Grampa knew what had happened,
He looked at the Man and started to cry.

He swore it happened that way,
A prophetic encounter of some kind;
A message sent from Heaven above,
That the Man won't be there for all time.

I'm not sure what happened that day,
But I know the Old Man's Spirit's here;
For when I visit the Old Man's mountain,
I can still feel his essence in the air.

Chapter 11

AN UNKNOWN LEGEND

Let's take a break from the Old Man,
I'll tell you a different story;
One, I know, you've not heard before,
Yes, I'm sane; so don't you worry.

There's pyramids in New Hampshire!
And they're quite a site to behold;
Older than the ones in Egypt,
One wonders what treasures they hold.

Legend has it that they were built,
Long before the Indians came;
Disguised to look more like mountains,
That's why they've garnered little fame.

They're not too far from the Old Man,
Southeast of the Indian Head;
Many have tried to get to them,
None have made it; all wound up dead.

Next time you're in the Granite State,
Be sure to come and have a look;
Don't bother checking in Rand-McNally,
This secret's not found in any book.

Not even the old timers up here,
Will ever help you in finding these;
I'll show them to you if you ask,
Long as you politely say please.

I'll take you where you can view them,
I'll show you any time you'd like;
The trail's not for the weak of heart,
So, be ready for one long hike.

But first, you must swear out an oath,
Not to tell anyone you've heard;
About our top secret pyramids,
But they exist; I give you my word.

They're to the east if you're looking north,
I see them nearly everyday;
And they still thrill me every time,
I pray that they aren't taken away.

Or the Indian Head for that matter,
It's sad enough that the Old Man's gone home;
But who's to say what the Spirit may do,
To steer us away from the path we're on.

Chapter 12

TRAIL OF AN OLD WARRIOR

Another legend tells us about,
An Indian chief hunting for game;
The old warrior wandered the notch,
All the day long until night time came.

Too late to walk back to his village,
He found a spot to spend the long night;
Beneath a rock ledge on the mountain,
He'd sleep under the pale moon light.

A snow storm blew in without warning,
Chilling the warrior to the bone;
Blowing snow enveloped the mountain,
The chief crawled deep under the stone.

Tired and hungry he soon fell asleep,
Dreams carried him through the valley;
Soaring above a summer landscape,
Teeming with birds and game a plenty.

When he awoke under the ledge,
Frozen stiff by the howling wind;
He felt his life slipping away,
But knew his Creator was with him.

And a voice spoke to him saying,
"It's here my Great Spirit will dwell;
Watch over all of my children,
Be sure that they are safe and well."

Then he became one with the mountain,
A sign placed up there for all to see;
That someone is watching over us,
Protecting those who long to live free.

Chapter 13

THE LEGEND OF A SAGAMORE

Not a Chief, but a Sagamore,
Fell in love with a Mohawk girl;
Thought to be bitter enemies,
White Dove chose to live in his world.

Together they lived happily,
There was peace because of their love;
Their tribes again were flourishing,
Blessed by the Great Spirit above.

One day her brother brought her news,
That their father would soon pass away;
He wished to see her one more time,
They needed to leave right away.

White Dove ran to her husband,
To tell him what was happening;
But the comfort of his strong arms,
Still couldn't stop her from crying.

"My father will soon be going,
To the Great Spirit in the sky;
He has asked to see me again,
Now I must go before he dies."

This brought sorrow to her husband,
For with his wife he could not go;
For an old battle injury,
Caused him to travel much too slow.

In his stead he sent warriors,
To guard her and act as her guide;
Until the day that she returned,
To once again be by his side.

Yet, he went with them as they left,
Traveled as far as he could go;
Until he could journey no more,
Their progress he didn't want to slow.

He drew her close and said goodbye,
Promising her he would not sleep;
Until she returned safely home,
To his arms to forever keep.

Then he returned to his people,
And kept himself busy to cope;
Thoughts of her danced within his mind,
On long nights he missed her the most.

When in dreams she would come to him,
Softly cooing much like a dove;
Telling him how much she missed him,
Reinforcing her tender love.

The summer passed by so slowly,
His dreams soothed his breaking heart;
Often he asked the Great Spirit,
"How much longer must we be apart?"

When her return was close at hand,
He returned to the very place;
Where long ago they'd said goodbye,
Longing again to touch her face.

But soon the days turned into weeks,
The harvest time had come and gone;
His smoke signals went unanswered,
Heart aching, he felt so forlorn.

Now winter storms were threatening,
The temperature dropped every day;
His braves built a shelter for him,
Until she returned, he would stay.

Now one of his braves spoke out to him,
Said, "You can't stay up here all alone;
A brave, fierce warrior you may be;
But you will not survive on this stone."

They knew he wouldn't change his mind
He was too determined to stay;
His love for his wife was so strong,
His thinking they could not sway.

They prepared to leave for their village,
But turned to bid him one more goodbye;
They were amazed by what they saw,
Sagamore's head filled the southern sky.

The Great Spirit immortalized him,
In what we knew as the Old Stone Face;
His essence forever to remain,
In this, a sacred Indian place.

Chapter 14

THE RETURN OF WHITE DOVE

When White Dove finally returned,
She didn't believe their story;
Of how Sagamore stayed behind,
It filled her heart with much worry.

With the braves who had gone with her,
She returned to where they parted;
They found the empty shelter there,
The truth left her broken hearted.

She told the braves that she would stay,
For her husband she must now weep;
And although they begged her not to,
She lied down, cried herself to sleep.

Her husband clearly spoke to her,
In the dream that she had that night;
Told her just how much he loved her,
How the Spirit would make things right.

How he would come down there to her,
Carry her to a special place;
Where they could ever be as one,
She slept with a smile on her face.

In the morning the braves found her,
Frozen like stone, she'd passed away;
But they knew that she had found peace,
So to the Great Spirit they prayed.

That the Sagamore and his wife,
Were as one in eternity;
Never again to be apart,
The hawk and his dove flying free.

Chapter 15

IN THE OLD MAN'S PRESENCE

It's said that many years ago,
An old Indian had an idea;
To capture the Old Man's favor,
A way to approach him without fear.

Years before, he had traveled south,
Learned of a remarkable weed;
With power to relax a stern man,
To make one kind and warm, indeed.

He had seen this happen himself,
When under its strange influence;
One sometimes told of secrets kept,
Where otherwise they had good sense.

He brought some back up north with him,
This strange weed they called tobacco;
Packed a quantity on his horse,
To see the Old Man he did go.

He arrived and said to himself,
"Now if I can bring him under;
The influence of this strange weed,
All of his knowledge I'll plunder."

He carved a great pipe from a root,
Of a tree that had fallen nearby;
He took some of the weed with him,
And started up the mountainside.

That day the wind was blowing right,
Into the face of the Old Man;
The perfect conditions to see,
If substance would come from his plan.

He blew some smoke from his own pipe,
The Old Man seemed to take it in;
His features seemed to mellow somewhat,
Was time for their talk to begin.

The Indian then showed him how,
To inhale and take a long toke;
After a few more instructions,
The Old Man blew a wreath of smoke.

They then talked for many hours,
Each taking turn with their stories;
And as they talked they smoked some more,
Putting aside all their worries.

Now we can readily suppose,
What their character might have been;
Perhaps they were about great storms,
The Old Man had seen way back when.

When the mountain was always covered,
By snow every day of the year;
When avalanches thundered down,
That filled the hearts of beasts with fear.

Of wonders which, from his sublime height,
He had seen in the heavens above;
How Indian children played below,
In the small lake created with love.

It's said they talked until nightfall came,
Time for the Indian to depart;
The Old Man wrapped himself in a cloud,
Content in having this heart to heart.

That night the Indian had a dream,
That filled him with worry and alarm;
Not a dream, but a premonition,
That something would bring his people harm.

Chapter 16

THE WARRIOR'S DREAM

The dream was about gatherings,
Of strange men who came to his land;
Filled with frightening explosions,
Raining destruction on his clan.

Devastating the great forests,
Bringing pollution all around;
Streams, lakes running red with blood,
Mighty monsters toiling the ground.

The howling of the wild beasts,
The strangest birds high in the sky;
Terrible visions so scary,
When he awoke, he started to cry.

He knew there was meaning in dreams,
And this one meant something indeed;
Thinking of it, it kept him awake,
It had a strange feeling of greed.

The only meaning he could make out,
Was pale faced men coming around;
Creating such havoc in his home,
Nowhere would peace ever be found.

In the name of what would be a State,
All of his land they would soon seize;
Done without caring, sense, or shame,
In quest for land, themselves to please.

They would then kill the wild animals,
That were his true companions and pets;
Then one day, destroy the Stone Face,
All the while, showing little regret.

Not knowing what he should now do,
He took a walk to the mountain;
The weather was bad, he was lost,
He wound up in what's called Lincoln.

He wandered up the wrong mountain,
Too tired to go on, he laid down;
Became one with the earth right there,
Forever as one with the ground.

Chapter 17

THE INDIAN HEAD

He became a wonder up here,
And although the Old Man is dead;
There's still a stone face on a mountain,
Better known as the Indian Head.

From the right spot in North Lincoln,
One may view the warrior clear;
A majestic stone face that shows,
God makes men in the mountains here.

About the time that 'pale face' came,
God placed this sign outside His door;
To tell our Indian brothers,
That after death there still is more.

Just like the Old Stone Face once was,
The Indian Head's a gift from above;
Sent down to us as a blessing,
No strings attached, just a gift of love.

Chapter 18

THE IMPRUDENT EAGLE

Now, there is another story,
If it is true, I just don't know;
A tale of a mother eagle,
That built her nest in the Old Man's nose.

How she ever dared to do this,
One cannot begin to imagine;
For the danger was very great,
One blow would send her down his mountain.

Must have been early one morning,
While the Old Man was still asleep;
When the nest was finally done,
She said, "Here's where my eaglets I'll keep.

"This place is sheltered from the storms,
And no one will think to hunt up here!"
So she laid her eggs in his nose,
Thinking she had nothing to fear.

All went well for a little while,
Until the first eaglet was born;
She flapped her wings with excitement,
That was her first mistake that morn.

For it tickled the Old Man's nose,
To the point he started to sneeze;
And she knew that if that happened,
It would be much worse than a breeze.

It would be very violent,
Throwing them down upon the rocks;
All who witnessed the Old Man sneeze,
Knew he probably lost his socks.

Rocks and trees would fly everywhere,
Wild beasts would scamper away;
The eagle screamed and woke him up,
That's how she saved their lives that day.

The next time you visit the notch,
Here is what I need you to do;
Find the oldest resident there,
Ask him if these stories are true.

You may be shocked by the answer,
For it is a matter of faith;
See for yourself; ask the Old Man,
His essence is here, it's not too late.

Chapter 19

ALL TRAILS LEAD TO HIS HOME

My trails may lead me far and wide,
But no matter where I may roam;
The one thing I know for certain,
All roads lead me back to his home.

I can't get him out of my head,
He's always with me in my heart;
Each new morning when I wake up,
I know a new trail's about to start.

I welcome them with open arms,
Knowing there's something new to learn;
New lessons I'm ever seeking,
For new wisdom my heart does yearn.

Today I'll go see the Old Man,
For his essence is always there;
He'll gladly teach me new lessons,
For this is how he shows he cares.

Take a walk with me to see him,
He'll welcome you with open arms;
In his presence you'll feel secure,
Make you feel that you're safe from harm.

The Old Man has never left me,
I keep him deep inside my mind;
For over the years I have found,
A better friend one cannot find.

At any given time of day,
Even at the drop of a hat;
He's always there when I need him,
I always know just where he's at.

Friends, the Old Man of the Mountains,
Can live inside each one of us;
All it takes is a leap of faith,
Walk with The Man that you can trust.

Chapter 20

AT HIS TRAIL'S END

He called Cannon Mountain his home,
But he's gone now, he's moved away;
Seeing what mankind had become,
He couldn't take another day.

The view all around was dazzling,
From high above his lake below;
From the ledge that was his front porch,
He watched man travel to and fro.

For countless years he held much hope,
That mankind would finally learn;
The teachings of The Great Spirit,
Seems so many would rather burn.

One day he found he'd had enough,
Mankind's future was looking bleak;
Love and compassion had left us,
Our hearts and souls were getting weak.

He really didn't have too much,
So he took what little he had;
Decided it was time to leave,
Yet, it still left him feeling sad.

"Great Spirit, I've been here too long,
I've tried to help them do things right;
But, they still ignore all your signs,
Their souls have lost the Spirits light.

"Now, if it is okay with You,
I would really like to come home;
I just can't look on anymore,
My heart's grown as cold as this stone."

The Great Spirit heard the Old Man,
Said, "Son, you may come home to me;
You'll be at peace forever more,
It's time for your soul to live free."

The sign that stood both day and night,
For more years than I care to count;
I mourn that your children won't see,
How he stood proudly on that mount.

But sure as the lightning will strike,
We'll remember all his glory;
And for those who choose to believe,
We'll continue to tell his story.

Of The Old Man that was a sign,
Sent by the Great Spirit above;
A sign that we should have followed,
To the Spirit's eternal love.

Yet, this mount still belongs to him,
Though he's left it and gone away;
His essence is still in the air,
In our hearts he will always stay.

The Man had many good reasons,
For leaving, though I question why;
Or was he simply showing us,
The meaning of LIVE FREE OR DIE !

Chapter 21

SHELTER FROM THE STORM

In the early eighteen hundreds,
He simply took a ride one day;
Through the notch in Franconia,
A fierce storm caught him on his way.

The temperature dropped rapidly,
As heavy snow started to fall;
He knew at once this meant trouble,
And he was not prepared at all.

He looked up through the blinding snow,
Suddenly saw The Old Man's face;
He and his horse against nature,
And nature was winning the race.

He knew he could trust The Old Man,
To the face he started to speak;
Knowing he didn't have much time,
He was rapidly growing weak.

"Great Spirit, I so need your help,
My horse and I are all alone;
Never thought that we'd hit a storm,
We're very far away from home.

"I've talked with you so many times,
Always heeded your sound advice;
Tell me exactly what to do,
Of your wisdom I won't think twice."

The Great Stone Face replied at once,
"Look to that rock in front of you;
One side is like a small shelter,
Listen, I'll tell you what to do.

"The only way that you'll survive,
Is to wedge yourself under that stone;
Kill your horse, wrap yourself in its hide,
I'll be with you, you'll not be alone.

So, Thomas Boise of Woodstock,
Did exactly as he had heard;
Survived the night through the storm,
He trusted in The Old Man's word.

With morning came a search party,
Wondering if he was still alive;
As they cut him from the frozen cocoon,
That was made from his horse's hide.

Today, the rock's still there to see,
Boise Rock as it's called today;
A gift of life from The Old Man,
To one whose faith showed him the way.

Chapter 22

THE WATCHER

Now many people have asked me, 'Where is The Old Man's loving wife?'
She's still here in the White Mountains, And she too, is bigger than life.

She's also known as The Watcher,
From a clearing near Profile Lake;
Look upward toward Eagle Cliff,
You'll be able to see her face.

She's a part of Mount Lafayette,
On the right of the highest pan;
The profile of The Old Lady,
As she was called within her clan.

She's facing east with her head bent,
Watching for people like me and you;
The smallest profile in the Notch,
Best to see in the afternoon.

Lately, she seems a little sad,
Welcomes visits by one and all;
I know she is a bit lonely,
Since her man left after his fall.

So, if you ever get the chance,
Or if you're just driving on by;
Take a moment, pay a visit,
To the Old Lady in the sky.

Chapter 23

PROFILES, BOULDERS and ROCK FORMATIONS

New Hampshire has many wonders,
Huge boulders and rock formations;
Some with distinct shapes and features,
Others take some imagination.

The Old Man was very distinct,
No question about that at all;
He has been very sadly missed,
Since the day that he took his fall.

His home was on Cannon Mountain,
Which in itself is a huge stone;
Almost resembling a fortress,
One cannon was close to his home.

The Old Lady sits to his north,
Some have said that she was his wife;
And not a word has she spoken,
Since the day that quake took his life.

Boise Rock lies below the place,
That the Old Man once called his home;
It is said to have saved a life;
A simple shelter made of stone.

Dewey Rock is just to the north,
It resembles the Admiral;
Found at the top of Artist Bluff,
Hope this stone never takes a fall.

Then there's the Sleeping Astronomer,
He can be found on Three O Two;
Reclining as he gazes at stars,
Near exit Forty One, see this view.

The Martha Washington stone head,
Look downstream and just to the right;
From the bridge on the Ammonoosuc,
George's wife is an awesome sight.

Then of course there's the Shining Rock,
Just hike the Falling Waters Trail;
It looks like a giant mirror,
Long as the spring waters don't fail.

And there's the great Elephant's Head,
One can view it from Crawford Notch;
The head's coming through the forest,
His trunk and all; I kid you not.

It's best seen from Crawford Depot,
By looking south down the Saco;
A huge gray rock with white quartz veins,
I bet of this one you didn't know.

And Pulpit Rock on the east side,
Of Carter Dome you can see it;
Partly detached from the cliff face,
Yes, it resembles a pulpit.

Of course there's a stone called The Sphinx,
See this one along the Sphinx Trail;
Between Mt. Jefferson and Mt. Clay,
Shortly before the Gulfside Trail.

Let's not forget the Imp Profile,
A profile in the Carter Range;
Best seen from the Dolly Copp Road,
This human head is very strange.

The two massive step like terraces,
These stairs gave Stairs Mountain its name;
Not as well known as the Old Man,
Giant Stairs could lead one to fame.

The next one's seen from the Glen House,
The Lion's Head, as it is known;
It was once called St. Anthony's nose,
On Route Sixteen near the Auto Road.

Of course there is George Washington,
A great boulder or just a rock?
This profile is on Thorn Mountain,
Though it looks more like Alfred Hitchcock.

Look for the Duck Head on a spur,
Just off Route Sixteen near Jackson;
Can be seen from nearby pastures,
Sitting atop Iron Mountain.

Still, I haven't told you of all,
The rocks and boulders one can find;
Like White Horse Ledge and Table Rock,
So many to boggle one's mind.

Davis Boulder and Goodrich Rock,
Glen Boulder and Cathedral Ledge;
Madison Rock and Index Rock,
Don't forget The Indian Head.

This one is known to very few,
I'll just call it The Monkey's Face;
Find it if you think that you can,
Near Jewel Hill he marks his place.

And there's America's Stonehenge,
In the southern part of the state;
So many things for one to see,
Just don't wait until it's too late.

You never know when they may go,
Just like the Old Man, they could leave;
Memories can't be taken away,
And these are here for you to receive.

Chapter 24

Even though The Old Man is gone, many still claim to have talked with him since the fateful day that he left us.
I offer you this tale as related directly to me by one of our troops who was home on leave from Iraq.
Take it for what it is worth. As for me? I believe !

A MODERN DAY LEGEND

A warrior traveled up north,
He was on a thirty day leave;
Glad to be away from the war,
Back home in the land of the free.

Something woke him early one day,
Told him he was to take a ride;
A voice said, "Come to my mountain,
I need you here now, by my side."

It was *The Old Man* calling him,
And he's always heeded his call;
It would be good to talk again,
Been awhile since they'd talked at all.

He parked just north of Profile Lake,
His essence he could clearly feel;
He glanced up at *The Old Man's* home,
The image he saw seemed so real.

If you knew *The Old Man* as he does,
You'd have no trouble believing;
That they still talk just like old times,
His messages have deep meaning.

The Old Man said, "There's no time to waste,"
His words were heavy with concern;
"Mankind must change its ways real soon,
Or like Sodom, the earth will burn.

"You people continue to hate,
You battle amongst each other;
Fighting for no reason at all,
Why must you kill your own brothers?

"Helpless children walk in harms way,
Innocent victims of madness;
They just ask to love and be loved,
It fills me with so much sadness.

"And you dare to ask why I left?
For years I watched your destruction;
It was your hate that drove me away,
You can't follow simple instructions.

"My friend, the time is drawing near,
Now is the time to make a choice;
The signs are all around you now,
Now it is time to hear my voice!

"Don't hesitate another day,
For tomorrow may be too late;
The choice is yours, you have free will,
It's you who will decide your own fate.

"Now pass this message on to all,
Don't you dare hold anything back;
Tell them *The Old Man* speaks the truth,
Tell them that I *only* speak fact.

"And if someone doesn't believe,
Send them directly here to me;
I'll see that they get my message,
I offer you peace and prosperity."

The warrior passed the words on,
Like before, they fell on deaf ears;
So in the misery of war,
We still battle year after year.

Chapter 25

A TEACHER OF STONE

A scene now only imagined,
High above a small lake below;
A sign unlike any other,
Placed up there so that all would know.

That in the state of New Hampshire,
Up in the mountains, God made men;
And people came from everywhere,
To make the Great Stone Face their friend.

Amid all of nature's wonder,
Seen against the clouds or the sky;
Stood a face, bold and beautiful,
It brought tears to many an eye.

With pines gently swaying below,
Birds gliding on currents above;
One could feel the Old Man's essence,
Filling their hearts and souls with love.

Called a silent philosopher,
Never known to utter a word;
Yet as a teacher we knew him,
In our hearts his lessons we heard.

No, it wasn't an accident,
That put him up there for all to see;
It was a power like no other,
And he gave us the will to live free.

Just rest in peace, teacher of stone,
Knowing some that you taught have learned;
The lessons you gave along the trail,
A special place in our hearts you've earned.

Chapter 26

A TRAIL OF REMEMBRANCE

He braved the thunder and lightning,
The harshness of the winters too;
He sat so high and majestic,
He was placed there for me and you.

Gazing down on us every day,
Protecting us through the long nights;
The Old Man of the Mountain cared,
He provided an awesome sight.

Been many years since he's been gone,
Still, I see his face way up high;
He's ever present in my heart,
Though his profile's gone from the sky.

New Hampshire doesn't feel the same,
With The Old Man of the Mountain gone;
It no longer feels like God's country,
Even the mountains seem so forlorn.

May Third will forever remain,
A special day of remembrance;
When we'll think about The Old Man,
And how much we miss his presence.

Chapter 27

ALIVE IN OUR HEARTS AND SOULS

Gone but never to be forgotten,
For he filled our lives with so much love;
A special place in our hearts we have,
For The Old Man sent down from above.

With his majestically etched stone face,
He had a look that was very stern;
But in our hearts we knew he was here,
To teach us lessons we needed to learn.

But only those with an open heart,
Knew just what he was sent here for;
Simply to spread the love he had,
We'll remember him forever more.

The Old Man of the Mountain was,
Alive in both our hearts and soul;
He's forever etched in our minds,
Ever with us as we grow old.

Made in the USA
Charleston, SC
28 August 2011